Do You Want a New Life?

'The Lord says, 'I will give you a new heart, and a new spirit.''

(Ezekiel 36:26)

D1563997

Peter Walker
www.1peter1three.weebly.com

To Tammy and Temple

And also to you, the reader

Introduction

Are you tired? Do you wish you could start life over again?

Do you wish you could take back things you said, and things you did?

Is your heart broken?

Have people hurt you, and you wish you could forget?

Have you hurt people, and you wish you could forget?

Jesus, who is God, has come to earth to save you. He took all of our sin and pain and hurt, and he died with it on the cross.

Jesus rose from the dead and offers you – *today* – a new life, a new start. He offers you forgiveness for your sin, and also healing from what others have done to you.

Do you want a new life?

Get Alone With God

We need to take a different path. We need to get alone with God.

Maybe today you will have a chance to do this. It is very simple, but can also be a hard choice to make.

For example, your friends might call you to go somewhere. It might not be a good idea to go. This is a perfect moment to choose a different path. You can simply stay home, or go somewhere else alone.

When we take a moment to get alone with God, Jesus will meet us there. But we have to *choose* to do it. We have to sacrifice something for it.

We have to say *'no'* to one thing, and *'yes'* to Jesus. We have to get alone with him on purpose.

Can you get alone with God? Where and when can you do that?

What can you say *'no'* to, so that you can get alone with God for a little while?

Jesus Meets You Here

When we take a moment to be alone with God, Jesus will meet us here by his Spirit.

Jesus came to give us **a new life**, and **a new path in life**. Do you want this? Do you need this?

It starts with your choice. You need to choose Jesus. You need to want the life he offers you.

You need to also be willing to stop doing things that you know are wrong, are sinful. This is called 'repentance'.

Are there things that you are doing, that you need to stop doing?

It can feel scary to stop doing things, or stop meeting people. It can feel lonely. But this is how we get alone with God. We step away from people and things that are not right. And here Jesus meets us by his Spirit.

Can you feel his Spirit with you now?

Let Jesus In

'Jesus said, 'I stand at your door and knock. If you hear my voice and open the door, I will come in.' (Revelation 3:20)

If you are ready to let Jesus in, here is a prayer you can pray to him now.

Prayer:

Dear Jesus, I need you. I need a new life. I need a new path in life. Please help me.

Jesus, I have done things that are wrong. I regret them. I ask you to forgive me for my sin. I ask you to help me to not do these things anymore. I ask you to give me a new path, your path.

Jesus, please heal my broken heart. Please give me a new spirit, a new heart.

Jesus, please open up to me a new way to go. Please help me meet other followers of Jesus, and to build a new life with you.

In Jesus' name I pray, amen and amen!

Taking Steps

My friend, if you have prayed and asked Jesus for his forgiveness, for his new life, he has saved you!

This is true, he promised it! Look at what he said:

'Jesus said, 'Whoever hears me and believes... they will not be judged, but they have crossed over from death to life.'
(John 5:24)

<u>You have crossed over into a new life in Jesus!</u>

Look at this verse, too:

'Jesus said, 'Come to me if you are tired and empty, and I will give you rest.'
(Matthew 11:28)

You have come to Jesus, and he is now with you. He has saved you. He has put his Spirit into you. He has made you his child.

'Because you are God's child, God has sent his Spirit into your heart.'
(Galatians 4:6)

Now it is time to start to <u>walk</u> on this new path of life with Jesus!

Trust

Now, my friend, the very first step to take, is a step of trust. You need to trust Jesus.

This is a deep thing. This is deep down in your heart.

You don't really know where Jesus is going to lead you, and maybe you are a little scared. For example, are you going to lose friends? Are you going to lose money or a place to stay?

Don't worry!

If you take steps on this new path of Jesus, he is with you.

So if you know you should not go somewhere today, or meet with some people, just don't! Stay where you are or go somewhere you can be with good people. Or just go somewhere you can be alone with God.

Jesus will bless you for this. Jesus will provide all you need – *food, shelter, good people.*

If you trust Jesus, and go his way, he will bless you.

Can you do this? Will you do this? Trust Jesus.

Say Sorry

Is there a good person you know – like a family member or friend – that could help you?

Maybe you need to say sorry to them for hurting them. Maybe you need to say sorry to them for stealing from them.

Sometimes there are people in our life, and they could help us now, but we have done wrong to them. So we think we have no one, but actually we just need to say sorry to some people. And if we did this, they would help us, they would be there for us.

Is there someone good in your life, someone you know loves you and you can trust? Is there someone you can go to and ask for help?

One time a guy told me he had no one, and no where he could go. But then he thought for a minute and said, *'Well, if I say sorry to my grandma, I know she would let me come stay.'*

I took him to his grandma's house. He apologized to her at the door, and she welcomed him in to start again.

Do You Need Help?

Maybe you have a problem with drugs? Maybe a problem with stealing, or sex and relationships?

Do you need to get clean? Do you need help?

I helped one lady get into a program that was going to be for 9 months. It took a month to get her into this program, and lots of money and time. She quit after 1 day. She just walked out and left. I lost a lot, and so did she.

Have people tried to help you, but you have wasted their help? Maybe you need to say sorry for this.

If you need help, you need to be the strong one to get it. You need to be 100% committed.

Jesus can give you this strength in your heart, in your body. If you pray and ask Jesus for the strength, he will give it.

And then you tell a friend, a family member, or a social worker or probation officer, that you are ready to get help. You are ready to get clean.

This is a big step. You can take it. Jesus is with you.

Time With God Every Day

Jesus is with you *ALL* day, every day. But we do need to set some time aside to be alone with him.

Every morning I get a cup of coffee, and sit quietly with Jesus for about 10 minutes. I read a little bit of the Bible, and I pray to him. I whisper to him. This is my special time with him.

Now, the rest of the day I am often praying to him. But that is different. That is time with Jesus '*on the road*', if you know what I mean.

It is important to find 5 or 10 minutes each day that you sit alone with Jesus for a special time with just him.

The next 10 pages are to help you do this. Each page gives you a verse to read, a space to write your thoughts, and a prayer to pray.

If you do these 10 pages over the next 10 days, you will see things happen in your life. You will get to know Jesus better, and see him move in your life.

Are you ready to go? Are you ready to grow? Do you have a pen ready?

OK, let's go…

Day 1: <u>TRUE PEACE</u>

'Jesus said, 'My peace I give you. It is different from the kind of peace the world gives.''
(John 14:27)

What are your thoughts on this verse? Write them here:

<u>Prayer</u>:

Dear Jesus, please give me your kind of peace. Please give me peace like a river in my soul. I need God's peace. In Jesus' name, amen!

Day 2: <u>REPENTANCE</u>

'Jesus said, 'If you love me, keep my commands.''
(John 14:15)

What are your thoughts on this verse? Write them here:

<u>Prayer</u>:

Dear Jesus, help me to obey your commands. Help me to turn away, to walk away, from wrong things and wrong people. In Jesus' name, amen!

Day 3: <u>CHURCH</u>

'Jesus said, 'Where 2 or 3 come together in my name, I am there with them.''
(Matthew 18:20)

What are your thoughts on this verse? Write them here:

<u>Prayer</u>:

Dear Jesus, help me to meet with other Christians every week. Help me to find a good church, and give me strength to go. In Jesus' name, amen!

Day 4: <u>**WISDOM**</u>

The Bible says, 'Work with your hands… so that you will not be dependent on anyone.' (1 Thessalonians 4:11-12)

What are your thoughts on this verse? Write them here:

<u>**Prayer**</u>:

Dear Jesus, please help me to find an honest job. Help someone to trust me, and give me a chance to work and earn a living. In Jesus' name, amen!

Day 5: **TRUSTWORTHY**

'Jesus said, 'Let your 'Yes' and your 'No' be honest and trustworthy.''
(Matthew 5:37)

What are your thoughts on this verse? Write them here:

Prayer:

Dear Jesus, help me to be honest. Help me to speak the truth so that people can trust me. In Jesus' name, amen!

Day 6: <u>HEALTHY MIND</u>

The Bible says, 'Whatever is true, whatever is noble, whatever is pure and lovely… think about these things.'
(Philippians 4:8)

What are your thoughts on this verse? Consider the things you watch online, you look at on your phone, the music you listen to… Write your thoughts here:

<u>Prayer</u>:

Dear Jesus, help me to look away from wrong things, to think and talk about true things, to fill my heart and mind with goodness. In Jesus' name I ask this, amen!

Day 7: <u>REST FOR YOUR SPIRIT</u>

'The Lord is my shepherd... He makes me lie down and rest. He leads me beside still waters. He restores my soul.'
(Psalm 23)

What are your thoughts on this verse? Write them here:

<u>Prayer</u>:

Dear Lord Jesus, thank you for giving me rest. Thank you for leading me to quiet places so I can be with you alone. In Jesus' name, amen!

Day 8: <u>**YOU ARE LOVED**</u>

God says about you, 'Before you were born I knew you. Before you were born, I set you apart. I have plans for you that are good!''
(Jeremiah 1:5; 29:11)

What are your thoughts on this verse? Write them here:

<u>**Prayer**</u>:

Dear Jesus, thank you for your love for me. Thank you for your good plans for me. I want to walk with you always. In Jesus' name I pray, amen!

Day 9: <u>ACTION!</u>

'Jesus said, 'Whoever puts my teaching into practice, is like a wise person who built their house on a strong foundation.''
(Matthew 7:24)

What are your thoughts on this verse? Write them here:

<u>Prayer</u>:

Dear Jesus, I want to get real about following you! I want to put my faith into action and build a strong life as a Christian. I ask for your help to do this, in Jesus' name, amen!

Day 10: <u>THE BIBLE</u>

'Jesus said, 'You are making mistakes because you do not know the Bible, together with the Spirit of God.''
(Matthew 22:29)

What are your thoughts on this verse? Write them here:

<u>Prayer</u>:

Dear Jesus, please help me to read the Bible and really understand it with the power of God. Make it easy for me to read, and help me remember it. I ask this in Jesus' name, amen!

Final Words

Do you need a Bible? I suggest going to a nearby church and asking them if they might give you one, or if you could pay for one.

Ask them for one that is easy to read.

Please take steps in following Jesus! Go to church every week if you can. Cut bad people out of your life. Cut bad 'content' out of your life – like pornography, bad movies, bad music.

Ask God to lead you to good people who follow Jesus. Read your Bible every day, pray, and worship. Get good worship music and listen, sing along.

Get a job that is good. Not a job at night or in an unsafe place, if you can.

Make good choices. Trust in Jesus. Walk with him. Pray and sing to him. His Holy Spirit is in you. You are a child of God now. He will lead you always.

God has promised,
'I will guide you always.'

(Isaiah 58:11)

For more information on following Jesus, please visit:

www.1peter1three.weebly.com

Write your thoughts and prayers here:

Write your thoughts and prayers here:

Write your thoughts and prayers here:

Write your thoughts and prayers here:

Write your thoughts and prayers here:

Write your thoughts and prayers here:

Made in the USA
Middletown, DE
07 April 2022

63783268R10019